As the Industrial Revolution spread wealth and work around Britain, a stronger and more influential middle class began to arise. And with it came a rise in social anxiety. For while nineteenth-century fashions were constantly changing, the importance of the baffling social codes was entirely rigid, and a newly prosperous and bewildered middle class was in dire need of careful guidance and advice.

And so rulebooks such as *Hints on Etiquette* began to emerge, aiming to demystify the byzantine laws governing behaviour and social interaction. Many of these pieces of advice might seem dated in the 21st century, but the popularity of *Downton Abbey*, the existence of hereditary peers and a fascination with the royal family are proof that the class system of Victorian Britain still casts its shadow today...

The books in "Found on the Shelves" have been chosen to give a fascinating insight into the treasures that can be found while browsing in The London Library. Now celebrating its 175th anniversary, with over seventeen miles of shelving and more than a million books, The London Library has become an unrivalled archive of the modes, manners and thoughts of each generation which has helped to form it.

From essays on sherry and claret to a passionate defence of early air travel, from advice on how best to navigate the Victorian dinner party to accounts of European adventures, they are as readable and relevant today as they were more than a century ago—even if it is no longer considered vulgar to lounge on sofas in the presence of ladies!

HINTS
on
ETIQUETTE

A Shield Against the Vulgar

The London Library

Pushkin Press

Pushkin Press
71–75 Shelton Street,
London WC2H 9JQ

Agōgós [i.e. Charles William Day], *Hints on Etiquette and the Usages
of Society: with a Glance at Bad Habits*. 22nd edition, revised (with
additions) by a Lady of Rank. London: Longman, Brown, Green, &
Longmans, 1842

Lewis Carroll, *Hints for Etiquette; or, Dining Out Made Easy*, 1849,
from *The Complete Works of Lewis Carroll*, with an introduction by
Alexander Woollcott and the illustrations by John Tenniel. London: The
Nonesuch Press, 1939

Illustrations from Albert Smith, *The Natural History of Evening
Parties*. London: D. Bogue, 1849

First published by Pushkin Press in 2016

9 8 7 6 5 4 3 2 1

ISBN 978 1 782273 21 9

Set in Goudy Modern by Tetragon, London

Printed by CPI Group (UK) Ltd, Croydon, CR0 4YY

www.pushkinpress.com

HINTS ON ETIQUETTE AND THE USAGES OF SOCIETY

with a Glance at Bad Habits

———— ⦉⦊ ————

BY AGOGOS, 1842

CHARLES WILLIAM DAY was a well-known painter of miniatures as well as the successful author of etiquette writings. *Hints on Etiquette*, which he wrote because he was "so distressed by the manners of the inhabitants of Hull", ran to 28 editions. He died in the second half of the nineteenth century, some time after the *Observer* had first reported his death.

Preface to the Nineteenth Edition

On my return to England after two years' incessant travel "from Dan to Beersheba," I found the usages "de la bonne société" somewhat changed: with a new *Reine*, new feelings and more refined observances had been introduced,—indeed I confess I should have felt slightly embarrassed, had not my ever attentive friend Lady —— kindly taken care of the interests of society during my absence, by noting whatever fluctuations had occurred, and that in so admirable a manner, that the instant adoption of her suggestions was as much a matter of duty as of gratitude. Yet, however curious the world may be to ascertain "which is the Leopard and which the Swan," it must ever remain a mystery between ourselves.

THE AUTHOR.

LONDON, OCTOBER, 1839.

Preface to the First Edition

This is not written for those *who do*, but for those who do *not know what is proper*, comprising a large portion of highly respectable and estimable people, who have not had an opportunity of becoming acquainted with the usages of the (so termed) "best society;" therefore, do not let the "select" sneer, and say—"Oh, every body knows *that*; there is nothing *new* here." Even *they* may be mistaken, and many may profit who will not choose to *own* how much they are indebted to this little book.

It would be absurd to suppose that those persons who constitute the upper ranks of the middle classes in LONDON are ignorant of the regulations here laid down;—but in the country (especially in the mercantile districts), where the tone of society is altogether lower, it is far otherwise, although country people may not feel inclined to acknowledge what is, nevertheless, strictly true.

If these "hints" save the blush but upon one cheek, or smooth the path into "society" of only one honest family, the object of the author will be attained.

LONDON, JAN. 20. 1836.

General Observations

Etiquette is the barrier which society draws around itself as a protection against offences the "*law*" cannot touch,—it is a shield against the intrusion of the impertinent, the improper, and the vulgar,—a guard against those obtuse persons who, having neither talent nor delicacy, would be continually thrusting themselves into the society of men to whom their presence might (from the difference of feeling and habit) be offensive, and even insupportable.

Many unthinking persons consider the observance of Etiquette to be nonsensical and unfriendly, as consisting of unmeaning forms, practised only by the *silly* and the idle; an opinion which arises from their not having reflected on the *reasons* that have led to the establishment of certain rules indispensable to the well-being of society, and without which, indeed, it would inevitably fall to pieces, and be destroyed.

Much misconstruction and unpleasant feeling arises, especially in country towns, from not knowing what is "*expected*," or necessary to be done on certain occasions, resulting sometimes from the prevalence of local customs, with which the world in general are not supposed to be acquainted.

Besides, in a mercantile country like England, people are continually rising in the world. Shopkeepers become merchants, and mechanics manufacturers; with the possession of wealth they acquire a taste for the luxuries of life, expensive furniture, gorgeous plate, and also numberless superfluities, with the use of which they are only imperfectly acquainted. But although their capacities for enjoyment increase, it rarely happens that the polish of their manners keeps pace with the rapidity of their advancement: hence such persons are often painfully reminded that wealth alone is insufficient to protect them from the mortifications which a limited acquaintance with society entails upon the ambitious. Pride often deters people from seeking the advice of the experienced, when the opportunity of receiving it is presented. It is to be hoped that the following remarks will furnish a guide through the intricacies of conventional usage, without risk to the sensitive, or the humiliation of *publicly* proclaiming the deficiencies of an imperfect education.

In all cases, the observances of the Metropolis (as the seat of refinement) should be received as the standard of good breeding.

Chap. I. – Introductions

Never "introduce" people to each other, without a previous understanding that it will be agreeable to both.

There are many reasons why people ought never to be introduced to the acquaintance of each other, without the consent of each party previously obtained. A man may suit the taste, and be agreeable enough to *one*, without being equally so to the *rest* of his friends—nay, as it often happens, he may be decidedly unpleasing; a stupid person may be delighted with the society of a man of learning or talent, to whom in return such an acquaintance may prove an annoyance and a clog, as one incapable of offering an inter-change of thought, or an idea worth listening to.

But if you should find an agreeable person in private society, who seems desirous of making your acquaintance, there cannot be any objection to your meeting his advances half way, although the cere-mony of an "introduction" may not have taken place; his presence in your friend's house being a sufficient guarantee for his respectability, as of course if he were an improper person he would not be there.

Should you, whilst walking with your friend, meet an acquaintance, never introduce them.

If you meet a male acquaintance giving his arm to a lady, take off your hat to him, instead of nod-ding—as this last familiar mode of recognition looks disrespectful towards *her*.

In making "introductions," take care to present the person of the lower rank to him of the higher; that is, the commoner should be presented to the peer, not the peer to the commoner; Dr. A. to Lord B., not Lord B. to Dr. A. Observe the same rule with ladies—the lady (as a female) claiming the highest rank, it is to *her* the gentleman must be presented, not the lady to the gentleman.

Be cautious how you take an intimate friend *uninvited* even to the house of those with whom you may be equally intimate, as there is always a feeling of jealousy that another should share your thoughts and feelings to the same extent as themselves, although good breeding will induce them to behave *civilly* to your friend on your account.

Friendship springs up from sources so subtle and undefinable, that it cannot be *forced* into particular channels; and whenever the attempt has been made, it has usually been unsuccessful.

Never make acquaintances in coffee-houses or other public places. As no person who respects himself does so, you may reasonably suspect any advances made to *you*.

An adherence to Etiquette is a mark of respect; if a man be *worth knowing*, he is surely worth the trouble to approach properly. It will likewise relieve you from the awkwardness of being acquainted with people of whom you might at times be ashamed, or be obliged under many circumstances to "*cut*."

The act of "*cutting*" can only be justified by some strong instance of bad conduct in the person

to be cut; a cold bow, which discourages familiarity without offering insult, is the best mode to
adopt towards those with whom an acquaintance
is not deemed desirable. An increased observance
of ceremony is, however, the most delicate way
of withdrawing from an acquaintance; and the
person so treated must be obtuse, indeed, who
does not take the hint.

A neglect of, or an adherence to, the forms of
society, in others towards yourself, is oftentimes
the only way in which you are enabled to judge if
your acquaintance be *really* considered desirable.
You will meet with professions of civility and
friendship in the world as mere matters of course;
and were you to act upon what people *say*, instead
of what they *do*, you would run a risk of being
mortified, which no person of proper pride would
choose to encounter; especially if the other party
be, or *assume to be*, of higher rank than yourself.
We never knew a person, really desirous of forming
a friendship with another, neglect, either by word
or deed, the means of accomplishing such an object.

It is, however, understood in society, that a
person who has been *properly* introduced to you,

has some claim on your good offices in future; you cannot therefore slight him without good reason, and the chance of being called to an account for it.

Chap. II. – Letters of Introduction

Letters of Introduction are to be considered as certificates of respectability——as proofs that you are known by the introducer to be a proper person to be admitted into the friendly circle of him to whom you are recommended, without the risk, in these days of elegant exterior, of his harbouring a swindler, or losing his silver spoons.

Many people consider that when they have given a dinner to the stranger they have done enough, and are not required to take any further notice of him, so that, with modern English coldness, "Letters of Introduction" have been facetiously termed "Tickets for Soup," and many sensitive people have, by these degrading considerations, been prevented from presenting them. It is true, that among people "*comme il faut*," the newcomer is generally welcomed with a dinner—not for the sake of the entertainment—but as a means of presenting him to a fresh society, and of giving him the opportunity of *legitimately* making the acquaintance of his host's friends invited expressly to meet him; but, as the only criterion of the estimation in which he is held must be the kind of people asked to meet him, be careful not to wound his feelings by inviting those whom he may be likely to consider his inferiors either in merit or position.

If you have letters of introduction from one friend to another, do *not take them*, but *send them*, with your card of address. If he be a *gentleman*, he will return your visit as soon as possible; at any rate it will give him an option, which by taking your letters in person you *do not do*, but rather force yourself upon him whether *he will or not*. If your letters be on business only, no ceremony is necessary—take them at once. In all such matters never trust to a *second* that which may be so much better done by yourself.

There cannot be a more awkward situation for both parties than for one person to be waiting whilst the other is reading a letter with the endeavour to discover who the stranger may be, or a position in which the bearer looks so foolish, or feels so uncomfortable. Then comes the bow, a cold shake of the hand, with the few civil words of course,—and all because you come upon a stranger who is unprepared: therefore give him time to read the letter you bring, and to consider how he may best show his regard for your introducer by his attentions to yourself.

Observe, that "Letters of Introduction" are never sealed by well-bred people: the seal of the writer is attached to the envelope—requiring only a little wax to close it,—at the option of the person to whom it is confided.

If a gentleman be the bearer of an "introduction" to *you*, leave a card with him without fail, if it be only as an acknowledgment of having received your friend's letter; there is no rudeness so great as to leave it unnoticed,—it is a slight to the stranger as well as to the introducer, which no subsequent attentions will cancel: you are not obliged to *invite* him, as *that* is a matter of choice.

In *France*, and indeed generally on the Continent, it is the established usage that strangers on arriving pay the first visit to residents. In England, with much better taste, the contrary is the rule. A stranger should never be made to feel that he is demanding attentions—but if possessed of true delicacy he would prefer waiting until they are offered. In spite of our own folly in occasionally copying them, the French (with a much greater *affectation of politeness*) are infinitely inferior to English gentlemen in true good-breeding.

Remember also, that a letter should never remain unanswered a moment longer than is absolutely unavoidable. Should you not have time to answer it *fully*, a simple acknowledgment is better than no notice of it at all.

An adherence to these rules will prevent your exposure to any coldness or slight you might otherwise incur.

Do not imagine these little ceremonies to be insignificant and beneath your attention; they are the customs of society; and if you do not conform to them, you will gain the unenviable distinction of being pointed out as an ignorant, ill-bred person. Not that you may *care* the more for strangers by showing them civility, but you should scrupulously avoid the imputation of being deficient in good-breeding; and if you do not choose to be polite for *their* sakes, you ought to be so for *your own*.

Chap. III. – Marriage

When a man marries, it is understood that all former acquaintanceship *ends*, unless he intimate a desire to renew it, by sending you his own and his wife's card, if near, or by letter, if distant. If this be neglected, be sure no further intercourse is desired.

In the first place—A bachelor is seldom *very particular* in the choice of his companions. So long as he is amused, he will associate freely enough with those whose morals and habits would point them out as highly dangerous persons to introduce into the sanctity of domestic life.

Secondly—A married man has the tastes of *another* to consult; and the friend of the *husband* may not be equally acceptable to the *wife*.

Besides—Newly-married people may wish to limit the circle of their friends, from praiseworthy motives of economy. When a man first "*sets up*" in the world, the burthen of an extensive and indiscriminate acquaintance may be felt in various ways. Many have had cause to regret the weakness of mind which allowed them to plunge into a vortex of gaiety and expense they could ill afford, from which they have found it difficult to extricate themselves, and the effects of which have proved a serious evil to them in after-life.

Chap. IV. – Dinners

Of the etiquette of a dinner party, it is extremely difficult to say any thing, because fashions are continually changing, even at the best tables; and what is considered the height of good taste one year, is declared vulgar the next; besides which, certain houses and *sets* have certain customs, peculiar to their own clique, and all who do not conform *exactly* to their methods are looked upon as vulgar persons, ignorant of good-breeding. This is a mistake commonly fallen into by the little "great"* in the country, where the circle constituting "*society*" is necessarily so small, that its members cannot fail to acquire the same habits, feelings, and observances. However, a few hints may not be thrown away, always recollecting that people can only become ridiculous by attempting to be *too fine*. I am, of course, supposing my readers to be acquainted with the *decencies* of life.

When the members of the party have all assembled in the drawing-room, the master or

---

* To avoid misconstruction, it will be as well to define what *is meant* by the term "little great," beginning by showing what is *not*.—It is NOT that numerous class (however respectable), professional and mercantile, found in and about every country town; those merely *great little*, who, without any other qualification than the possession of a few thousand pounds, constitute themselves the aristocracy of the place: but a very different body,—namely, the old, solid, "COUNTY PEOPLE," the descendants of patrician families, the Squirearchy, with incomes of from seven to ten thousands a year, and the customary representatives in parliament (until lately) of their town or county,—persons who are of great *local influence* and importance, on account of their descent and wealth, but who, notwithstanding, become insignificant and merely *units in the mass*, amidst the brilliant statesmen, the talent, the splendour of rank and fashion which adorn and elevate the metropolis.

mistress of the house will point out which lady you are to take into the dining-room, according to some real or fancied standard of precedence, rank (if there be rank), age, or general importance; that is, the married before the single, &c.; or they will show their tact, by making companions, those who are most likely to be agreeable to each other. Give the lady the wall coming down stairs, take her into the room, and seat yourself by her side.

If you pass to dine merely from one room to another, offer your left arm to the lady.

* Remember that it is the lady who at all times takes precedence, not the gentleman. A person led a Princess out of the room before her husband (who was doing the same to a lady of lower rank); in his over-politeness, he said, "Pardonnez que nous vous précédons," quite forgetting that it was the *princess* and not *he* who led the way.*

Well-bred people arrive as nearly at the appointed dinner hour as they can. It is a very vulgar assumption of importance purposely to arrive half an hour behind time; besides the folly of allowing eight or ten hungry people such a tempting opportunity of discussing your foibles.

The lady of the house will of course take the head of the table, and the gentleman of the highest rank will sit at her *right* hand; the gentleman next in rank will be placed on the left of the

---

* Of those passages marked with an asterisk, the groundwork has been taken from the MS. note-book of a lady of rank.

hostess, so that she may be supported by the two persons of the most consideration (who will assist her to carve).

In many houses of distinction, the master and mistress sit *vis-à-vis* to each other at the middle of the table.

In nearly all the houses of the nobility, at present, the operation of carving is performed at the side table, where the *pièce de résistance*, by which is meant the roast joint, is placed.

It is the custom at present for the lady of the house to *follow* her guests into the dining-room, except when a prince of the royal family is present, who leads out the lady of the house first.

The gentleman of the house takes the bottom of the table, and on each side of *him* must be placed *the two ladies highest in rank*. You will find a party of *ten* convenient, as it admits of an equal distribution of the sexes: neither two men nor two women like to sit together.

It is a matter of regret that table napkins are not considered indispensable in England; for, with all our boasted refinement, they are far from being general. The comfort of napkins at dinner is too obvious to require comment, whilst the *expense* can hardly be urged as an objection. If there be not any napkins, a man has no alternative but to use the table-cloth, unless (*as many do*) he prefer his pocket handkerchief—an usage sufficiently disagreeable.

It is considered vulgar to take fish or soup twice. The *reason* for not being helped twice to fish or soup at a large dinner party is—because by doing so you keep three parts of the company staring at you whilst waiting for the second course, which is spoiling, much to the annoyance of the mistress of the house. The selfish greediness, therefore, of so doing constitutes its vulgarity. At a family dinner it is of less importance, and is consequently often done.

Do not ask any lady to take wine, until you see that she has *finished* her fish or soup. This exceedingly absurd and troublesome custom is very properly giving way at the best tables to the more reasonable one of the gentleman helping the lady to wine next to whom he may be seated, or a servant will hand it round. But if either a lady or a gentleman be invited to take wine at table, they must *never refuse*; it is very *gauche* so to do. They need not drink half a glass with each person, but merely taste of it.

Asking ladies to take wine is now quite exploded. It is merely offered by the gentlemen who sit next to them; but if you are in a country house where the custom is retained, it would be better breeding to follow the fashion of the place, rather than, by an omission of what your enter-tainer considers civility, to prove him, in the face of his guests, to be either ignorant or vulgar.

It is considered well bred to take the same wine as that selected by the person with whom you drink, the choice being left to the person highest in rank, or most advanced in age. When, however, the wine chosen by him is unpalatable to you, it is allowable to take that which you prefer, prefacing it with, "Will you permit me to drink claret, sherry," &c.

At every respectable table you will find *silver* forks; being broader, they are in all respects more convenient than steel for fish or vegetables. Steel forks, except for carving, are now never placed on the table.

At family dinners, where the common household

bread is used, it should never be cut less than an inch and a half thick. There is nothing more plebeian than *thin* bread at dinner.

NEVER *use your knife to convey* your food to your mouth, *under any circumstances*; it is unnecessary, and glaringly vulgar. Feed yourself with a *fork* or *spoon, nothing else,*——a knife is only to be used for cutting.

If at dinner you are requested to help any one to sauce, do not pour it over the meat or vegetables, but on one side. If you should have to carve and help a joint, do not load a person's plate—it is vulgar: also in serving soup, one ladleful to each plate is sufficient.

Fish should always be helped with a silver fish-slice, and your own portion of it divided by the fork aided by a piece of bread.

The application of a knife to fish is likely to destroy the delicacy of its flavour; besides which, fish sauces are often acidulated; acids corrode steel, and draw from it a disagreeable taste. In the North, where lemon or vinegar is very generally used for salmon and many other kinds of fish, the objection becomes more apparent.

Eat PEAS with a dessert spoon; and curry also. Tarts and puddings are to be eaten with a *spoon*.*

As a general rule—in helping any one at table, never use a knife where you can use a spoon.

Making a noise in chewing, or breathing hard in eating, are both unseemly habits, and ought to be eschewed.

Many people make a disgusting noise with their lips, by inhaling their breath strongly whilst taking soup—a habit which should be carefully avoided.

  *   *You cannot use your knife, or fork, or teeth too quietly.*

Do not *press* people to eat more than they appear to like, nor *insist* upon their tasting of any particular dish: you may so far recommend one, as to mention that it is considered "excellent." Remember that tastes differ, and viands, which please *you*, may be objects of dislike to *others*; and that in consequence of your urgency, very

---

* By a step in pseudo refinement, the etiquette of 1839 pronounces that the use of a spoon for these purposes must be carefully avoided at dinner, it being only admissible for soup and ices.

young or very modest people may feel themselves compelled to partake of what may be most disagreeable to them.

* Do not pick your teeth *much* at table, as, however satisfactory a practice to yourself, to witness it is not at all pleasant.

Ladies should never dine with their gloves on—unless their hands are not fit to be seen.

Servants occasionally wait at table in *clean white gloves*: there are few things more disagreeable than the thumb of a clumsy waiter in your plate.

The custom, however, of servants waiting at table in gloves, has never been adopted in the mansions of people of distinction. A white damask napkin, in which his thumb is enveloped, is given to each servant, and this effectually precludes its contact with your plate.

Glass wine-coolers, half filled with water, should be placed next each person at table.

Finger glasses, filled with *warm* water, come on with the dessert. Wet a corner of your napkin, and wipe your mouth, then rinse your fingers; but do not practise the *filthy* custom of gargling your

mouth at table, albeit the usage prevails amongst a few, who think that, *because* it is a foreign habit, it cannot be disgusting.

The custom of drinking toasts, and of forcing people to drink bumper after bumper of wine, until drunkenness results, is quite banished from *gentlemanly society* to its proper place—the tavern. It arises from a mistaken idea of making visitors welcome: the Amphitryon of the feast overlooking the fact of its being *much more hospitable* to allow his guests to do as they please, and to take only as much wine as they may feel convenient or agreeable. It is but a miserable boast, that a man has sufficient strength of stomach to sit his companions "under the table."

* Never pare an apple or a pear for a lady unless she desire you, and then be careful to use your fork to hold it: you may sometimes offer to *divide a very large pear* with or for a person.

At some of the best houses, coffee is brought into the dining-room before the gentlemen quit the table—a very good custom, as it *gently* prevents excess, the guests retiring to the ladies immediately afterwards; it also allows those who have other engagements to take coffee before they quit the house. Coffee should be brought in at an hour previously appointed, *without the bell being rung for it*, but a sufficient interval must be allowed, lest the host seem chary of his wine. For instance, nine o'clock is a good hour, if the dinner were at six; or ten o'clock for one which commenced at seven.

At present, coffee is not brought into the dining-room in fashionable houses, except when a small party, intending to go to a theatre, are pressed for time—it is always served in the drawing-room. Nevertheless, the former is a very excellent arrangement in *country houses*, for very obvious reasons.

Coffee, *on the Continent*, and sometimes in England, is followed by liqueurs of two or three kinds, which are left to the choice of the guests, and are poured into very small glasses—an unnecessary custom, not to be advocated in *respectable*, but only in "*high*" society.

Do not suppose that it will exalt you in the opinion of others, by speaking harshly and imperatively to servants, or add at all to your consequence. Never order other people's servants about. At a strange table, say "if you please," and "thank you:" it may be said in a manner that will not encourage familiarity.

Should your servants break any thing while you are at table, never turn round, or inquire into the particulars, however annoyed you may feel. If your servants betray stupidity or awkwardness in waiting on your guests, avoid reprimanding them *publicly*, as it only draws attention to their errors, and adds to their embarrassment.

Nothing indicates a well-bred man more than a proper mode of eating his dinner. A man may pass muster by *dressing well*, and may sustain himself tolerably in conversation; but if he be not perfectly "au fait," *dinner* will betray him.

It is a piece of superlative folly for men who dine at a house to take their round hats into the drawing-room: it answers no purpose at all; and the necessity of giving them to a servant on enter-ing the dinner room, creates confusion. Men of fashion, nevertheless, invariably take their hats into the drawing-room, where they are left when people go to dinner, and whence they are removed by the servants, and placed in the ante-room, or vestibule.

Invitations to dine should be answered to the lady. Invitations to a ball should be in the lady's name, and the answer of course sent to her.

It is customary, when you have been out dining, to leave a card upon the lady the next day, or as soon after as may be convenient.

Attentions of this sort are not to be expected from professional men, as Doctors, Lawyers, &c., *their* time being too valuable to sacrifice in making visits of mere ceremony; therefore, do not attribute such omission to any want of respect, but to its proper cause—*time more usefully occupied.*

When a man is about to be married, he usually gives a dinner to his bachelor friends; which is understood to be their congé, unless he choose to renew their acquaintance.

Chap. V. – Smoking

If you are so unfortunate as to have contracted the low habit of smoking, be careful to practise it under certain restrictions; at least, so long as you are desirous of being considered fit for civilised society.

The first mark of a gentleman is a sensitive regard for the feelings of others; therefore, smoke where it is least likely to prove personally offensive by making your clothes smell; then wash your mouth, and brush your teeth. What man of delicacy could presume to address a lady with his breath smelling of onions? Yet tobacco is equally odious. The tobacco smoker, in *public*, is the most selfish animal imaginable; he perseveres in contaminating the pure and fragrant air, careless whom he annoys, and is but the fitting inmate of a tavern.

Smoking in the streets, or in a theatre, is only practised by shop-boys, pseudo-fashionables— and the "SWELL MOB."

All songs that you may see written in praise of smoking in magazines or newspapers, or hear sung upon the stage, are *puffs*, paid for by the proprietors of cigar divans and tobacco shops, to make their trade popular,—therefore, never believe nor be deluded by them.

Never be seen in cigar divans or billiard rooms; they are frequented, at best, by an equivocal set. *Nothing good* can be gained there—and a man loses his respectability by being seen entering or coming out of such places.

Chap. VI. – Snuff

As snuff-taking is merely an idle, dirty habit, practised by stupid people in the unavailing endeavour to clear their stolid intellect, and is not a custom particularly offensive to their neighbours, it may be left to each individual taste as to whether it be continued or not. An "Elégant" cannot take *much* snuff without decidedly "losing caste."

"Doctor," said an old gentleman, who was an inveterate snuff-taker, to a physician, "is it true that snuff destroys the olfactory nerves, clogs, and otherwise injures the brain?" "It cannot be true," was the caustic reply, "since *those who have any brains never take snuff at all*."

Chap. VII. – Fashion

But few things betray greater imbecility of mind than a servile imitation of the extravagancies of any fashionable monster. A man possessed of the delicate and proper feelings of a gentleman would deem himself *degraded* by copying another, even to the curling of a whisker, or the tie of a cravat; as, by so doing, he could only show the world of how little importance he felt himself, and the very poor opinion he entertained of his own taste.

Fashion and *gentility* are very distinct things—for which reason, people, *really* of the highest rank, are too proud to become martyrs to any prevailing mode; and the man of true taste will limit his compliance with the caprices of fashion to not appearing *equally conspicuous* for its utter neglect.

Chap. VIII. – Dress

It is bad taste to dress in the extreme of fashion; and, in general, those only do so who have no other claim to distinction,—leave it, in these times, to shopmen and pickpockets. There are certain occasions, however, when you may dress as gaily as you please, observing the maxim of the ancient poet, to be "great on great occasions." Men often think when they wear a fashionably cut coat, an embroidered waistcoat, with a profusion of chains and other trinkets, that they are well dressed, entirely overlooking the less obtrusive, but more certain, marks of a refined taste. The grand points are—well-made shoes, clean gloves, a white pocket handkerchief, and, *above all*, an easy and graceful deportment.

Do not affect singularity in dress, by wearing out-of-the-way hats, or gaudy waistcoats, &c. and so become contemptibly conspicuous; nothing is more easy than to attract attention in such a manner, since it requires neither sense nor taste. A shrewd old gentleman said of one of these "ninnies," that "*he would rather be taken for a FOOL, than not be noticed at all.*"

A dress perfectly suited to a tall good-looking man, may render one who is neither ridiculous; as although the former may wear a remarkable waistcoat or singular coat, *almost* with impunity, the latter, by adopting a similar costume, exposes himself to the laughter of all who see him. An unassuming simplicity in dress should always be preferred, as it prepossesses every one in favour of the wearer.

Never affect the "ruffianly" style of dress, unless, as some excuse, you hold a brilliant position in society. A nobleman, or an exceedingly elegant and refined man, is sometimes foolish enough to disguise himself, and assume the "ruffian," as it amuses him to mark the surprise of people at the *contrast* between his *appearance* and his *manners*; but if *you* have no such pretensions, let your costume be as unostentatious as possible, lest people only remark that "your *dress* is as *coarse* as your *mind*."

Always wear your gloves in church or in a theatre.

Avoid wearing jewellery, unless it be in very good taste, and then only at proper seasons. This is the age of mosaic gold and other trash; and by dint of swindling, anyone *may* become "flashy" at a small expense. Recollect that every shop-boy can coarsely imitate your "outward and visible sign" if he choose to save his money for that purpose. If you *will* stand out in "high and bold relief," endeavour to become eminent for some virtue or talent, that people may say, "There goes the *celebrated* (not the *notorious*) Mr. So-and-so."

It is a delicate subject to hint at the incongruities of a lady's dress,—yet, alas! it forces itself upon our notice when we see a female attired with elaborate gorgeousness, picking her steps along the sloppy streets, after a week's snow and a three days' thaw, *walking* in a dress only fit for a carriage. When country people visit London, and see a lady enveloped in ermine and velvets, reclining in a carriage, they are apt to imagine it is the fashionable dress, and adopt it accordingly, overlooking the coronet emblazoned on the panels, and that its occupant is a duchess or a marchioness at the least, and that were the same person to *walk*, she would be in a very different costume, and then only attended by a footman.

Ladies of good taste seldom wear jewellery in the morning; and when they do, confine themselves to trinkets of gold, or those in which opaque stones only are introduced. Ornaments with brilliant stones are unsuited for a morning costume.

Chap. IX. –
Of Music in General Society

It is the misfortune of musical people generally to be such enthusiasts, that, once beginning, they seldom know when to leave off: there are few things a greater *seccatura* than a long "Concerto," or duet upon the pianoforte, or an

"Air with (endless) variations." The listeners get fidgety and tired, although they are usually too polite to say so. I once sat next to a foreigner, who had endured with exemplary patience a tedious "Concerto," and who, when it was finished, applauded vehemently, then, turning round to me with a droll expression of countenance, said, "*perchè si finisce*."*

Nothing, however, is more rude than to converse whilst people are singing. If you do not like music sufficiently to listen to it, you should remember that others may do so, and that not only do you interrupt their enjoyment of it, but you offer an offence to the singers.

A song *now* and *then* is very desirable, as it is a relief to conversation, but half a dozen consecutively, even from St. Cecilia in person, would become a bore; besides which, people are now accustomed to hear popular songs executed by those whose profession it is, with a superiority rarely attainable in private life, so that amateurs seldom do more than provoke unfortunate

---

* "Because it's finished."

comparisons. However, when highly-gifted musicians *are* found in private society, we have generally observed their *delicacy* to be in proportion to their *excellence*.

But the case is much worse when a professional "violinist" is admitted into a private party: he either flourishes away, unconscious that he is not in an orchestra, or else, desirous to prove his superiority over the "*dillettanti*," he overpowers them with a tone which might fill a cathedral. The best fiddles *scream* too much in (comparatively) small rooms, however delicately they may be played; besides that few even of the first English musicians seem to understand what an "*accompaniment*" really means, each performer

being too intent on making his particular instrument heard above the rest, to care about the *subject*, or to feel that an "accompaniment" should be subdued, and *subservient* to the voice.

We once heard the silver tones of an exquisite singer completely overpowered, between the shriekings of a fiddle, the vainglorious grumblings of a violoncello, and the wheezings of a dyspeptic flute.

Chap. X. – Dancing

With the etiquette of a ball-room, so far as it goes, there are but few people unacquainted. Certain persons are appointed to act as stewards, or there will be a "master of the ceremonies," whose office it is to see that every thing be conducted in a proper manner: if you are entirely a stranger, it is to *them* you must apply for a partner, and point out (quietly) any young lady with whom you should like to dance, when, if there be no obvious inequality of rank, they will present you for that purpose; should there be an objection, they will probably select some one they consider more suitable; but do not, on any account, go to a strange lady by yourself, and request her to dance, as she will unhesitatingly "decline the honour," and think you an impertinent fellow for your presumption.

Any presentation to a lady in a public ball-room, for the mere purpose of dancing, does not entitle you to claim her acquaintance afterwards; therefore, should you meet her the next day, do not attempt to address her. At most, you may lift

your hat; but even that is better avoided,—unless, indeed, she first bow,—as neither she nor her friends can know *who* or *what* you are.

In France, Italy, Germany and Russia, gentlemen invariably take off their hats to every lady in whose society they had ever previously been, even though no introduction had taken place; but they do not consider themselves authorised to address a lady in conversation to whom they have not been presented. This is surely the usage most consistent with true politeness towards women.

Do not wear *black* or coloured gloves, lest your partner look sulky; even should you be in *mourning*, wear *white* gloves, not *black*. People in DEEP *mourning* have no business in a ball-room at all.

LEAD the lady through the quadrille; do not *drag* her, nor clasp her hand as if it were made of wood, lest she not unjustly think you a boor.

You will not, if you are wise, stand up in a quadrille without knowing something of the figure; and if you are master of a few of the steps, *so much the better*. But dance quietly; do not kick and caper about, nor sway your body to and fro:

dance only *from the hips downwards*; and lead the lady as lightly as you would tread a measure with a spirit of gossamer.

Do not pride yourself on doing "steps neatly," unless you are ambitious of being taken for a dancing-master; between whose motions and those of a *gentleman* there is a great difference.

If a lady should civilly decline to dance with you, making an excuse, and you chance to see her dancing afterwards, do not take any notice of it, nor be offended with her. It might *not* be that she *despised you*, but that she *preferred another*.

We cannot always fathom the hidden springs which influence a woman's actions, and there are many bursting hearts within white satin dresses; therefore do not insist upon the fulfilment of established regulations "de rigueur." Besides, it is a hard case that women should be compelled to dance with every body offered them, at the alternative of not being allowed to enjoy themselves at all.

If a friend be engaged when you request her to dance, and she promises to be your partner for the next or any of the following dances, do not neglect her when the time comes, but be in readiness to fulfil your office as her cavalier, or she may think that you have studiously slighted her, besides preventing her obliging some one else. Even inattention and forgetfulness, by showing how little you care for a lady, form in themselves a tacit insult.

If a lady waltz with you, beware not to press her waist; you must only lightly touch it with the open palm of your hand, lest you leave a disagreeable impression not only on her *ceinture*, but on her mind.

Above all, do not be prone to quarrel in a ball-room; it disturbs the harmony of the company, and should be avoided, if possible. Recollect that a thousand little derelictions from strict propriety may occur through the *ignorance* or *stupidity* of the aggressor, and not from any intention to annoy: remember, also, that *really well-bred* women will not thank you for making them conspicuous by over-officiousness in their defence, unless, indeed, there be any serious or glaring violation of decorum. In small matters, ladies are both able and willing to take care of themselves, and would prefer being allowed to overwhelm the unlucky offender in their own way.

If, while walking up and down a public promenade, you should meet friends or acquaintances whom you do not intend to join, it is only necessary to salute them the *first time of passing*; to bow or to nod to them every round would be tiresome, and therefore improper; do not be afraid that they will think you odd or unfriendly, as, if they have any sense at all, they will appreciate your reasons. If you have any thing to say to them, join them at once.

Chap. XI. – Conversation

Many men of talent forget that the object of conversation is to entertain and amuse, and that society, to be agreeable, must never be made the arena of dispute. Some persons spoil every party they join by making it their only object to prove that every one present is in the wrong but themselves.

49

It requires so much tact and good breeding to sustain an argument, however logical and correct the arguer may be, that an avoidance of it will gain him more popularity than a triumph over his adversary could accomplish.

Even slight inaccuracy in statement of facts or opinions should rarely be remarked on in conversation.

A man should never permit himself to lose his temper in society—not *show* that he has taken offence at any supposed slight—it places him in a disadvantageous position—betraying an absence of self-respect,—or at the least of self-possession.

If a "puppy" adopt a disagreeable tone of voice—or offensive manner towards you—*never resent it at the time*—and above all do not adopt the same style in your conversation with him; appear not to notice it, and generally it will be discontinued, as it will be seen that it has failed in its object, besides which—*you save your temper*.

* Be careful in company how you defend your friends, unless the conversation be addressed to yourself. Remember that nobody is perfect, and people may sometimes speak the truth; and that, if contradicted, they may be desirous of justifying themselves, and will *prove* what might otherwise have been a matter of doubt.

Wit elicits wit; and when such brilliant materials meet, they form the flint and steel of conversation: appreciation is the tinder, which, though not bright in itself, receives and cherishes the scintillations as they fall. Who has not felt his intellect expand with the assurance of having what he says understood? Appreciation certainly *is a talent*.

Never "talk *at* people"——it is in the worst possible taste, as it is taking an unfair advantage of them: if there be any thing you dislike, "*out with it boldly*," and give them an opportunity of explaining, or of defending themselves,——or else *be silent*.

* Do not say a person is "affable" unless he or she be of very high rank, as it implies condescension. ROYAL *personages* are "gracious."

* Do not repeat the name of the person to whom you are speaking, as,——"Indeed, Mr. Stubbs, you don't say so, Sir,"——or, "Really, Mrs.

Fidkins, I quite agree with you, Mrs. Fidkins." It is a sufficiently bad habit in an equal, but in one of lower rank it becomes an impertinence.

In talking of *your own children*, never speak of them as "*Master* William," or "*Miss* Jane;" "*Mr.* Henry," or "*Miss* Louisa:" it is a miserable attempt to elevate both them and yourself, which will assuredly fail, as it is practised by those only who have *recently* risen above that dingy mass of mediocrity—"the multitude;" leave it, therefore, to others to pay them so proper a mark of respect, secure that none but *very intimate friends* will take the liberty of calling them plain "Mary" or "Edward:" this is an important caution, as it is generally the first error committed by the "*nouveaux riches*."

Above all things, do not mistake stiffness for dignity; the very spirit of good breeding consists in being easy and natural yourself—and in the endeavour to make others the same. Etiquette is only the *armour* of society; and when your position is fairly established, it may be thrown aside, at least so far as is consistent with good feeling and decorum.

Avoid a loud tone of voice in conversation, or a "horse laugh:" both are exceedingly vulgar; and if practised, strangers may think that you have been "cad" to an omnibus. There is a slightly subdued *patrician tone of voice*, which we fear can only be acquired in good society. Be cautious also how you take the lead in conversation, unless it be forced upon you, lest people reiterate the remark made on a certain occasion upon that "*Brummagem*" Johnson, Doctor Parr,—that "he was like *a great toe* in society; *the most ignoble part of the body, yet ever thrust foremost.*"

Be very careful how you "show off" in strange company, unless you be thoroughly conversant with your subject, as you are never sure of the person next to whom you may be seated. It is a common occurrence for young gentlemen of very shallow pretensions indeed, to endeavour to astonish country society, never dreaming that experienced London men *may* be present, when an exposure most probably follows as a penalty for their presumption. For instance—never talk largely of the "Opera,"—"Pasta, Grisi, Lablache," &c. on the strength of having been there once or twice only, lest you unwittingly address some old frequenter of the theatre, who has for the last twenty years been accustomed to hear all the "*Primi cantanti, serii e buffi,*" and who will, most likely, have every opera, its "casts," and music, at his tongue's end: neither talk learnedly of pictures,—"bits," "effects," or of "masters,"—"Titian," "Rubens," &c. from the very slight information to be obtained from copies or engravings, for fear some sly old fellow, who is conversant with all the "collections" from "Dan to Beersheba," should be malicious enough to *analyse* your knowledge; indeed, as the consciousness of ignorance is apt to make people peculiarly sensitive, it would be as well to avoid all subjects with which *you know* the generality of persons present *cannot be acquainted*; for, as the mere introduction of such topics will be considered and resented as an assumption on your part, should you happen to be vanquished on your own ground, your defeat will be relished proportionably. Remember, that if *you are quiet in society*, you will, at least, have credit for discretion, and be more likely to escape annoyance;

it is display alone that courts publicity and provokes criticism. It would astonish and frighten the mock brilliants we so often meet, could they but know how quickly and infallibly the practised eye will detect their position in the world, in spite of the gaudy lacker spread over (in the hope of concealing) a homely material; in such cases, gorgeous vestments act but as conductors to the coarse shirt, and clumsy ill-made boots—such *as a gentleman could not wear*; the vulgar pronunciation *of one word*—or an awkward *undrilled walk*, is sufficient to render more than doubtful the legitimacy of the most captivating exterior.

It is a matter of observation, that there are so few people who know how to *walk* properly, and who do not "get along" with a lounging "*slewing*" gait; also the many pseudo "militaires," who appear never to have known, that to carry themselves erect—to step well—*and to turn out their toes*—are amongst the earliest and most indispensable preparations for a military life.

There cannot be a custom more vulgar or offensive than that of taking a person aside to whisper in a room with company, yet this rudeness is of frequent occurrence—and that with persons who ought to know better.

Lounging on sofas, or reclining in chairs when in society, as if in the privacy of one's own dressing room or study, is always considered indecorous; but in the presence of ladies is deemed extremely vulgar.

There are but few things that display worse taste than the introduction of professional topics in general conversation, especially if there be ladies present: the minds of those men must be miserably ill-stored, who cannot find other subjects for conversation than their own professions. Who has not felt this on having been compelled to listen to "clerical slang," musty college jokes, and anecdotes divested of all interest beyond the atmosphere of an university; or "law" jokes, with "good stories" of "learned counsel;" "*long yarns*;" or the equally tiresome muster-roll of "our regiment"——colonels *dead*, maimed majors retired on pensions, subs lost or "exchanged," gravitating between Boulogne and the King's Bench?——All such exclusive topics are signs either of a limited intellect, or the most lamentable ignorance.

Making the "sports of the field," or anecdotes of the clubs, the topics of conversation in female society, will subject a man to the imputation of having a very *mauvais ton*; indeed, people should be careful not to introduce topics that have only a local interest, and not to speak slightingly of those who are the friends of any of the guests.

Mothers should be on their guard not to repeat nursery anecdotes or *bon-mots*, as, however interesting to themselves, they are seldom so to others.

Long stories should always be avoided, as, however well told, they interrupt general conversation, and leave the impression that the narrator thought the *circle* dull, and consequently endeavoured to amuse it.

An exceedingly vulgar custom prevails in the northern part of England,—that of women using the titles of their husbands as marks of distinction to themselves; being spoken of, or written to, and even having printed on their cards, "Mrs. *Capt. Gubbins*," "Mrs. *Dr. Borax*," or the more balmy and euphonious appellation of "Mrs. *Col. Figgins*" (generally the flaxen-haired owner of a bilious Colonel, from "Choultry Plains," and late of Cheltenham). It springs from a desire to show the world how much they are exalted by their husbands' rank above the "Muggs" and "Jenkinses" of low life. How oddly "Mrs. *Alderman* Tibbs," or "Mrs. *Churchwarden* Hobbs," would sound! To such an extent is this desire for *title* carried, that at Aberdeen a row of dram-shops near the Pier is placarded as being kept by "Mrs. *Captain* Gordon," "Mrs. *Captain* M'Dougal," &c., being the consorts of the "masters" of the trading smacks. The proper mode of distinguishing the wives of various members of the same family is by using the *Christian* name; as Mrs. Edward, Mrs. James, &c., as the case may be.

Never use the term "*genteel*." Do not speak of "*genteel people*;" it is a low estimate of good breeding, used only by vulgar persons, and from *their* lips implies that union of finery, flippancy, and affectation, often found in those but one remove from "hewers of wood and drawers of water." Substitute "*well-bred person*," "*manners of a gentlewoman*," or of "*a gentleman*," instead.

Never use the initial of a person's name to designate him; as "Mr. P.," "Mrs. C.," "Miss W.," &c. Nothing is more abominable than to hear a woman speak of her husband as "Mr. B."

In speaking to ladies of title, do not say "my lady," it being only proper for servants and tradespeople so to do; you may occasionally say "your ladyship," as it shows that you are aware of their claim to the distinction.

The fear of being thought vulgar often drives meritorious people, who have risen by their own exertions, into the opposite extreme, and causes them to be superlatively delicate. Such persons are shocked at the sound of "*breeches*," will substitute "inebriated" for "*very drunk*," and cannot be brought to allow there are such animals as "*women*" in the world.

It is also a clumsy attempt at refinement to use a particular *set* of words: at present we have "*splendid* travelling," "*splendid* gin," "*splendid* potatoes," &c.

Chap. XII. – Advice to Tradespeople

By tradespeople I do not mean merchants or manufacturers, but shopkeepers and retailers of various goods, who will do well to remember that people are respectable in their own sphere only, and that when they attempt to step out of it *they cease to be so*. When exceptions are made by the world, it is generally in favour of brilliant genius or extraordinary acquirements, and, even then, it can only be by the prevailing suffrage of society; therefore do not attempt to claim the acquaintance of those above you, lest you meet a mortifying repulse. Many will say, "We are just as good as they are, and as respectable." SO YOU ARE, but yet not fit companions for each other. Society is divided into various orders, each class having its own views, its peculiar education, habits, and tastes; so that the conversation of the one would probably be most uninteresting to the other. It is the fashion to talk of the spread of education—and, so far as merely reading and writing go, it is true; but they are only the *first steps* to a cultivated mind, and the literary acquirements of a man of business are necessarily confined to reading the newspaper. *He has no time for any thing else*; and, however skilful in his trade, cannot form an idea of that *man's mind* who has devoted all his energies to science or literature. Nay, can you suppose that even the merchant of Portland Place and the occupant of the back parlour to a butcher's shop think and feel alike? Certainly not; and recollect also, that however highly *you may estimate yourself*, the *world* will judge you by any standard rather than your own.

The English are the most aristocratic democrats in the world; always endeavouring to squeeze through the portals of rank and fashion, and then slamming the door in the face of any unfortunate devil who may happen to be behind them.

Chap. XIII. – Visiting

If you are thrown amongst fashionable people, you must not pay a visit to a lady before three o'clock P.M., nor after five, as, if you call *before* that time, you will interrupt those avocations which more or less occupy *every lady* in the early part of the day: if *later* than five o'clock, you will prevent her driving out.

On returning visits, a card left at the house is generally considered all that is necessary; but, if you are admitted, do not make a morning visit too long, lest you interfere with the engagements of the mistress of the house.

* Never leave your hat in the hall when you pay a morning visit; it makes you look *too much at home*; take it with you into the room.

Chap. XIV. — Visiting Cards

When a family arrive in London, they should send out cards to their acquaintances to inform them of that event, as well as of their address.

The names of the daughters who have been presented are to be inscribed on the cards of their mothers.

One card is sufficient for a mother and daughters to leave, and should there be daughters or sisters residing with the lady called on, the corner or corners of the card may be turned down, to signify that the visit is meant for them also.

When a married lady makes a call, she may leave her husband's card.

It is not unusual for persons to send cards by their servants to return visits; but this mode is considered disrespectful, excepting when it is to return thanks for "inquiries."

On the Continent, persons inscribe on their cards "*en personne*," to show that they themselves have come, and not *sent* their cards. Many of the English, regardless of the motive, notwithstanding its being so evident, had the same words written on theirs, and the persons to whom these cards were sent not unfrequently had cards with "*en personne*" thrust into the hands of their porter by a *laquais de place*, when they were in the vestibule, or entering their carriages, which excited much laughter, the *servants* also joining in the mirth.

When a wedding takes place in a family, the cards of the newly married pair are sent round to all their acquaintances to apprise them of the event. The cards are sent out by the bridegroom to his acquaintances, and by the parents of the bride to theirs. In some instances the cards have been united by silken or silver cords, but this mode has not been adopted by people of fashion.

To those who leave cards at the residence of the bride and bridegroom during their absence in the "honey moon," cards are sent to inform them of their return.

When cards are left for married people who reside with their parents or relatives, their names should be written on the cards left for them to preclude mistakes.

When persons without parents are married, they should send their cards to their acquaintances.

Foreign ladies always inscribe their maiden names, as well as their married ones, on their cards—as, " La Comtesse de M—— *née* de S——"; this explains to what family they belong, and prevents mistakes where there are others of the same name. An English lady observing this mode, and wishing to adopt it, left her cards with the following inscription, "Mrs. Popkins— *née* Tibbetts," to the no small amusement of the quizzer with whom they were left.

In giving dinners, endeavour to engage persons only who are known to each other, or who mutually desire to become acquainted. Exceptions may be made in favour of persons of acknowledged merit, or of high distinction.

In society, verbal invitations are often given to balls or concerts, by persons with whom you are only slightly acquainted, and have not previously visited: in such a case, it is proper to leave a card beforehand on the lady at whose house the soirée is to take place, that she may be made acquainted with your name and intention—so that you may be expected; because you may have received an invitation from her husband of which she was ignorant, and he may not be there to present you. Should it so occur, a card previously left will prevent either party looking foolish, or the stranger appearing "de trop."

Some doubts having arisen, after a death, as to the proper period of returning cards of "thanks" for visits of condolence, we believe there is no fixed time; for, as cards of thanks imply that the bereaved parties are prepared to receive visitors, it must be, with them, *entirely a matter of feeling*.

In *France*, deaths, births, and marriages are announced by unsealed letters sent round by the heads of the family in which the event has occurred. These are called "*lettres de faire part*." Those addressed to relatives are written by the *chef de famille*; and those to friends and acquaintances are printed.

Chap. XV. – Cards

Card-tables are generally set out in a room appropriated to their use, or else in the room of reception, where they are placed apart. When coffee has been served, the master or mistress of the house proposes cards to the visitors, and those disposed to play advance to the table, at which a fresh pack of cards is opened, and spread, and each person intending to play draws a card. The persons who draw the highest card are *excluded* from the rubber; but the four individuals who have drawn the lowest, again draw cards for partners; the two highest become partners; and the two who have drawn the lowest have the choice of seats and the deal.

At the commencement of every fresh rubber the players again cut for partners. For the regulation of the games, our readers are referred to Major A*****'s "Hints on Whist." Wagers are made in preference with the persons playing; but if they decline to accept them, a player is justified in betting with any of the spectators.

In *good* society it is considered *mauvais ton* to be too punctilious and exacting with regard to the penalties incurred through mistakes, which, in general, are only enforced at the Clubs, where "play" is looked on as an affair on the stock exchange; where each individual profits by the indiscretion of his opponent. To *lose* without any exhibition of ill-humour, and to *win* without any symptom of exultation, are deemed characteristic of high breeding and *savoir vivre*, and those who cannot always remember this, would do well to give up play.

Women should never play except for trifling sums, and not even then, unless they can retain the command of their temper; she who wishes to win a heart, or to retain one, should never permit her admirers to behold her at cards, as the *anxiety* they produce is as destructive to beauty as to sentiment.

Chap. XVI. – Tattling

It has somewhere been observed that, "In good society, a tacit understanding exists that whatsoever conversation may take place shall be to a certain degree sacred, and may not honourably be carried out of it, and repeated to the prejudice of the utterer." This axiom cannot be too strongly inculcated; as, if such practices were allowed, all confidence would be destroyed, and there would be no end to the mischief caused by silly or malignant people.

Conversations ever *have* taken place, and ever *will*, in which opinions are given, and motives scrutinised, truly and justly too, and with decided advantage to the world, as it is very often the only way in which one half of mankind can be put upon their guard against the other; nevertheless, but few people would be pleased to learn that their designs, their foibles, or their weaknesses,

had been made the subject of discussion, as most men flatter themselves the world will take them at whatever value they may choose to set upon themselves. There are none, therefore, so despicable, as those traitors to society who hurry from house to house, laden with the remarks made by one party upon another; stirring up discord and strengthening hatred wheresoever they appear,—by whom every unguarded expression is distorted or magnified, and who take a malicious pleasure (too often under the guise of affection) in wounding one friend at the expense of another. This is the bane of country society, and falls particularly heavy on those "accustomed to all the freedom of thought and frankness of expression of a great capital, and who find it difficult, if not impossible, to adopt the caution so necessary in a small community."*

Consequently, give *your own opinion* of people if you choose, but you are not at liberty to repeat that of others. Only fancy the result of one lady saying to another, "Well, Maria, what do you

---

* Life of Mackintosh.

think Miss Macaw says of YOU? She says, that you have the thickest ankles, and the thinnest arms, of any girl in the county; with a *contour* like an *Alligator*, and a head like a *Bison*!!!"

Be cautious how you indulge in *badinage* in the presence of dull, common-place people; they will either get out of temper in consequence of taking what you say literally, or else will stare and wonder at you for being such a "strange man." "Poor Susan!" said a gentleman to a pretty girl. "Poor, indeed!" replied the lady, with an indignant toss of the head; "not so poor as *that* comes to. Papa can give us something."—What an anticipation for the sensitive aspirant!

Chap. XVII. – Of General Society

If you meet a lady of your acquaintance in the street, it is *her part* to notice *you first*, unless, indeed, you are very intimate. The reason is, if *you* bow to a lady first, she may not choose to acknowledge you, and there is no remedy; but if *she* bow to *you*—you, *as a gentleman, cannot cut her*.

On the Continent the fashion in this instance as in many others, is exactly the reverse. No lady, however intimate you may be with her, will acknowledge your acquaintance in the street, unless you are the first to honour her with a bow of recognition. It must be obvious, however, to all thinking persons, that our own custom is the most in accordance with good taste.

Never *nod* to a lady in the street, neither be satisfied with touching your hat, but *take it off*,—it is a courtesy her sex demands.

Never keep your hat on when handing a lady to her box or to her carriage.

Never slam the door of a box with violence, nor speak loudly enough to disturb an audience. When you visit a lady in her box at the opera, be sure to leave it when other visitors enter, lest you be *de trop*.

Never sit in the boxes of a theatre with your *hat on*; it is an insult to the rest of the audience, especially if there be ladies.

*   Do not insist upon pulling off your glove on a very hot day when you shake hands with a lady. If it *be off*, why, all very well; but it is better to run the risk of being considered ungallant, than to present a *clammy* ungloved hand.

Never, indeed, offer your hand, unless well assured that it is in a presentable state of frigidity; for the touch of a tepid hand chills the warmest feelings.

On entering a coffee-house, and sitting down, *take off your hat*; it is only a proper mark of respect to your own class, towards whom you should pay the same deference you exact from others.

If you meet a friend in the street—in a coffee-house, shop, or indeed *any* public place, never address him by name; at least, not so loudly as that others may hear it: sensitive people do not like to be "shown up" to strangers as "Mr. Jones," or "Mr. Smith," and so attract disagreeable notice. Accost your friend *quietly*; and do not *roar out*, "Ah! Mr. Smith! how do you do, Mr. Smith?" it is very offensive, and shows a great want of proper delicacy.

Do not *strain* after great people,—for, although they like the homage, inasmuch as it flatters their vanity, yet they despise the dispenser of it. Pay them, however, all proper respect; but do not forget what is due to yourself.

As a general rule—it is the place of the superior in rank to speak first to the inferior.

When presented to a person of high rank, you should leave a card at his house the next day.

If you have been in society with a nobleman, and should chance to meet him again elsewhere, leave it to him to speak first, or to recognise you. If *you* claim *his* acquaintance, you give him an opportunity of behaving superciliously to you, which would be as well avoided.

An unfortunate Clerk of the Treasury, who, because he was in the receipt of a good salary, besides being a "triton amongst the minnows" of Clapham Common, fancied himself a great man, dined at the B—f S—k Club, where he sat next to a noble Duke, who, desirous of putting him at ease with himself, conversed freely with him, yet probably forgot even the existence of such a person half an hour afterwards. Meeting his Grace in the street some days after, and encouraged by his previous condescension, the hero of the quill, bent on claiming his acquaintance, accosted him in a familiar "hail fellow-well-met-ish" manner,—"Ah, my Lord, how d'ye do?" The Duke looked surprised. "May I know, Sir, to *whom* I have the honour of speaking?" said his Grace, drawing up. "Oh ! why—don't you know? We dined together at the B—f S—k Club, the other evening!—I'M MR. TIMMS OF THE TREASURY!!" "Then," said the Duke, turning on his heel, "MR. TIMMS OF THE TREASURY, I wish you *a good morning*."

Remember that all your guests are equal for the time being, and have a similar claim to your courtesies; nay, if there be a difference shown, those of the lesser rank require a *little more attention* than the rest, that they may not be made to *feel* their inferiority.

There is no more common or absurd mistake than supposing that, because people are of high rank, they cannot be vulgar;—or that, if people be in an obscure station, they cannot be well bred. We have seen as many instances of vulgarity in a peer as could be found in a grazier; and have noticed as many examples of a perfect freedom from the least taint of it in persons in humble life, as could be desired in a duchess.

Nothing more clearly indicates the true gentleman than a desire evinced to oblige or *accommodate*, whenever it is possible or *reasonable*; it forms the broad distinction between the well-bred man of the world, and the coarse and brutal crowd—the irreclaimably vulgar,—vulgar, not from their inferiority of station, but because *they are coarse* and *brutal*. Nevertheless, we often find persons so selfish and supercilious, and of so equivocal an importance, that they fancy any compliance with the wishes of the many, would tend to lessen their dignity in the eyes of their companions, and who foolishly imagine that a good coat places them above the necessity of conciliating the feelings of the multitude by the performance of an act of courtesy. It is evident there cannot be a greater mistake, since even the lower classes (whatever their own practices may be) keenly appreciate, and gratefully acknowledge, the slightest consideration shown to them by their superiors. That persons should be found weak enough to believe themselves above control, is lamentable, as such silliness can only expose them to the ridicule of their equals, and the contempt of their superiors.

A perfect freedom from affectation, and an observance of the feelings of others, will always exempt a person from the charge of vulgarity.

Be careful to offer a favour in such a manner as not to offend the delicacy of those whom you wish to serve. Favours may be so conferred as to become insults. If kindness and a desire to oblige induce you to offer an "attention," do not *press* it after it has been once refused, and so affront ill-tempered or testy people. A friend who had been dining a short distance from London, when about to return, said to one of the party, "Sir, my carriage is at the door; if agreeable, I shall be happy to take you to town."—"I am much obliged to you," replied the ungracious Mr. Tubbs, drawing himself up, "but—*I have a carriage of my own.*"

When you offer a place in your carriage, be sure to give the best, or you will subject yourself to the charge of ignorance and ill-breeding.

* Do not cross a room in an anxious manner, and force your way up to a lady merely to receive a bow, as by so doing you attract the eyes of the company towards her. If you are desirous of

being noticed by any one in particular, put your-self in their way as if by accident, and do not let them *see* that you have sought them out; unless, indeed, there be something very important to communicate.

* Do not take upon yourself to do the hon-ours in another man's house, or constitute your-self master of the ceremonies, as you will thereby offend the host and hostess.

There is a shallow attempt at "fallen great-ness," sometimes practised by persons who wish it to be supposed they are below their proper sphere,—that of bestowing high-sounding titles upon very ordinary objects; as calling a hack-ney-coach "the carriage;" or speaking of a gig, or wretched pony chaise, as "our carriage;" or of a miserable passage, three feet wide, as the "hall." This is very foolish, and does not impose upon any one.

In addressing letters to persons of rank, the *title* should be written, whether of Duke, Marquis, Earl, Viscount, or Baron, instead of "Lord" So-and-so, which is considered disrespectful and vulgar. This rule should be particularly attended to in writing to Ladies, in order to avoid confounding the rank they hold with the very inferior one of the wives of Baronets or Knights. *Military* rank always takes precedence of titles on the superscription of letters.

As the term "*Esquire*" has long degenerated into a title of mere courtesy, be careful to give it when writing to any person above the rank of a shopkeeper, and scrupulously award it to all professional men; *not to do so*, would appear like an ungracious attempt, on your part, to depreciate them, and to display *your own importance* by affecting to under-rate *their pretensions*; besides, as the first lesson taught to "people of condition" is "to be courteous to all men," and as you will rarely find these little proprieties overlooked *by them*, any neglect on your part will naturally suggest the inference, that the offending epistle was indited by some very *assuming* or very *ignorant* person. It is needless in these times to consider the distinctions made by the "Law" in ages past; for as "belted knights" exist no longer, the *reality* of an Esquire has long merged in the shadowy *title*, which, "*as by law allowed*," is shared by the lowest pettifogger, or the coarsest tradesman admitted into the ranks of the "Gentlemen pensioners."* We do not attempt to deny that "Esquire," in common with the terms "Professor," or "Professional," is occasionally abused, since a "Professorship" rewards alike

---

* Gentlemen pensioners are Esquires by "authority." This ancient and pleasant provision for decayed gentlemen was much distorted during the last reign, by the admission of improper persons; so conspicuous, indeed, did its squalidness and vulgarity become, as to attract the attention, and excite the ire, of the late sovereign, who threatened to disband such an equivocal appendage to his state. The institution has now, however, become regenerate, by restricting the *quality* of its members; and at present shines forth in more than its pristine splendour, as the "Honourable Band of Gentlemen-at-Arms,"— so be it.

the saltatory labours of a dancing master, and gilds the graceful avocations of an "*Arcadian*" hairdresser.

In writing to subalterns in the army, be careful not to address your letter to *Ensign* or *Lieut.* So-and-so, but to J. P. *Esq.*, 83d Reg^t., &c., as the case may be; *Captain* being the lowest grade which a military man chooses to acknowledge.

Do not offer a person the chair from which you have just risen, unless there be no other in the room.

Never take the chair usually occupied by the mistress of the house, even though she be absent, nor use the snuff-box of another, unless he offer it.

Do not touch any of the articles of *bijouterie* in the houses where you visit: they are meant only for the use of the lady of the house, and may be admired, but not touched.

Do not beat the "devil's tattoo," by drumming with your fingers on a table; it cannot fail to annoy every one within hearing, and is the index of a vacant mind. Neither read the newspaper in an audible whisper, as it disturbs the attention of those near you. Both these bad habits are particularly offensive where most common; that is, in a country news-room. Remember, that a carelessness as to what may incommode others is the sure sign of a coarse and ordinary mind; indeed, the essential part of good breeding is more in the avoidance of whatever may be disagreeable to others, than even an accurate observance of the customs of good society.

Never allow any person above the rank of a shopman to leave the room without your ringing the bell for the street door to be opened. Thousands have been irremediably offended by having been suffered to quit a room unattended, and to "let themselves out." This deserves particular notice, as it is a very common omission with persons, who, having amassed a little wealth and set up for "*somebodies*," would be exceedingly annoyed to have it whispered that they could be guilty of such gross ill breeding.

People who have risen in the world are too apt to suppose they render themselves of consequence *in proportion to the pride they display*, and their want of attention towards those with whom they come in contact. This is a terrible mistake, as every ill-bred act recoils with triple violence against its perpetrators, by leading the offended parties to analyse them, and to question their right of assuming a superiority to which (in the absence of *positive rank*) they are but rarely entitled.

People who may be what, in French phraseology, are termed *parvenus*, or *nouveaux riches*, and who desire to attain a good position in society, must be careful to avoid making any advances to people of rank, and should wait until these last seek their acquaintance. A contrary line of conduct will only draw on them the imputation of forwardness and vulgarity. For as it is the privilege of the person of the highest rank to make the first advances towards acquaintanceship, there is no excuse for the inferior to commit himself.

Do not abuse the advantage of a "twopenny post," by making people pay the postage of letters on *your own* business merely, and transmitted through such a channel entirely for your convenience, by saving the trouble of sending a servant. The postage upon one solitary note is small, it is true; but may amount to a large sum in the aggregate. Depend upon it, the most "*tiffy*" people will not be very much offended at the postage being paid, although some affect *openly* to despise an expense at which they grumble in *secret*.

There is no better test of a man's claim to be considered "a gentleman" than a scrutiny of his conduct in money transactions. A man may possess rank and fashion, and, by an assumed frankness of character, deceive the multitude; but the moment his purse is invaded, if he be not of the true caste, he will display the most contemptible meanness, he will take advantage of the liberal— *evade*, by every miserable subterfuge, the claims of those he dares not oppress, and unblushingly *defy* those unfortunate persons whose poverty is likely to prevent the due assertion of their rights. Such a man may possess station in society—he may be an "élégant"—he may be a *prince*! but, *if he be not honest—he is not a gentleman.*

With intimate friends, you may dispense with ceremony as much as may be deemed desirable to all parties; but with strangers, or persons with whom you are only imperfectly acquainted, every deviation from established custom *is a slight*, as it tends to show how little their society is appreciated; and will (if they possess a grain of spirit) be resented accordingly.

Although these remarks will not be sufficient in themselves to *make* you a *gentleman*, yet they will enable you to avoid any glaring impropriety, and do much to render you easy and confident in society.

Gentility is neither in birth, manner, nor fashion—but in *the* MIND. A high sense of honour—a determination never to take a mean advantage of another—an adherence to truth, delicacy, and politeness towards those with whom you may have dealings—are the essential and distinguishing characteristics of *a* GENTLEMAN.

HINTS FOR ETIQUETTE

or, Dining Out Made Easy

BY LEWIS CARROLL, 1849

CHARLES LUTWIDGE DODGSON, the author, mathematician and photographer, is best known as the writer of *Alice's Adventures in Wonderland* and *Through the Looking-Glass, and What Alice Found There*. He grew up in "complete seclusion from the world", teaching himself logarithms and befriending animals. Dodgson moved to Oxford in 1851, and stayed there until his death in 1898.

As caterers for the public taste, we can conscientiously recommend this book to all diners-out who are perfectly unacquainted with the usages of society. However we may regret that our author has confined himself to warning rather than advice, we are bound in justice to say that nothing here stated will be found to contradict the habits of the best circles. The following examples exhibit a depth of penetration and a fullness of experience rarely met with:

I

In proceeding to the dining-room, the gentleman gives one arm to the lady he escorts—it is unusual to offer both.

II

The practice of taking soup with the next gentleman but one is now wisely discontinued; but the custom of asking your host his opinion of the weather immediately on the removal of the first course still prevails.

III

To use a fork with your soup, intimating at the same time to your hostess that you are reserving the spoon for the beefsteaks, is a practice wholly exploded.

IV

On meat being placed before you, there is no possible objection to your eating it, if so disposed; still, in all such delicate cases, be guided entirely by the conduct of those around you.

V

It is always allowable to ask for artichoke jelly with your boiled venison; however, there are houses where this is not supplied.

VI

The method of helping roast turkey with two carving-forks is practicable, but deficient in grace.

VII

We do not recommend the practice of eating cheese with a knife and fork in one hand, and a spoon and wine-glass in the other; there is a kind of awkwardness in the action which no amount of practice can entirely dispel.

VIII

As a general rule, do not kick the shins of the opposite gentleman under the table, if personally unacquainted with him; your pleasantry is liable to be misunderstood—a circumstance at all times unpleasant.

IX

Proposing the health of the boy in buttons immediately on the removal of the cloth is a custom springing from regard to his tender years, rather than from a strict adherence to the rules of etiquette.

"FOUND ON THE SHELVES"

THE LONDON LIBRARY (a registered charity) is one of the UK's leading literary institutions and a favourite haunt of authors, researchers and keen readers.

Membership is open to all.

Join at www.londonlibrary.co.uk.

www.pushkinpress.com